AFGE:

ANOTHER F*ING GROWTH EXPERIENCE

Pronounced

AF as in "after" and GE as in" glee"
(but get the "L" out of there!)

BARBARA H. WHITFIELD and **SHARON K. CORMIER**

ENDORSEMENTS

AFGEs offers both wisdom and practicality from two near-death experiencers. But to attribute this wisdom solely to their NDEs would shortchange their incredible journeys since their NDEs – Barbara's through the psychology of trauma survivors and Sharon's through yoga and Buddhist tradition. Combining these two paths, they show us how we can use AFGEs to move out of ignorance and into knowing who we really are. Barbara and Sharon help us through profoundly simple techniques to explore the fears behind our AFGEs and to emerge from these challenges healthy and grateful.

Bruce Greyson, MD Director, Division of Perceptual Studies, University of Virginia Health System

AFGE is a perfect word to highlight those moments and situations I'd prefer to bury -- *if* peace, joy and contentment weren't the rewards I want in my life. Using each AFGE as a launching pad helps me be even more willing to sideline the survival tools of drama/trauma/chaos *I had* to build during a childhood lived in family dysfunction. Barbara and Sharon's book is the *HOW-TO* we need!! I offer it as an easy-to-follow handbook for clients I serve in early recovery.

Just saying 'AFGE' brought me more quickly to a deeper level of consciousness!

Gail M. Ross, Ph.D.
Palm Beach, Florida

**BARBARA AND SHARON IN BARBARA'S KITCHEN IN THE
GREENHOUSE, NEWINGTON, CONNECTICUT 1989**

We (Sharon and Barbara) met at a support group meeting for
Near-Death Experiencers (IANDS: The International Association
for Near-Death Studies) in 1985. We became fast friends and
even shared a two family flat that was 100 years old with
slanted floors, windows that wouldn't open and plumbing on
the outside of the walls. To add to the experience, it was painted
a dull institutional green inside and out! Along with our three
teenage sons, we affectionately called it the "Greenhouse."

APRIL 1990. HERE WE ARE ON LARRY KING LIVE
TALKING ABOUT OUR NEAR-DEATH EXPERIENCES

We didn't have much money but had a lot of fun laughing at life and growing psychologically and spiritually from all our shared AFGEs. Now for the first time ever, we share the wisdom we gained from diving into our AFGEs and coming out on the other side into a life enriched with joy and clarity.

SKC & BHW

AFGE
Another F*ing Growth Experience

A Guide to Self-Awareness and Change.

BARBARA WHITFIELD and SHARON CORMIER

GreenHouse Press
Is an imprint of
MuseHouse Press
Atlanta, Georgia
2013

Authors photo by Steve Cartano of Cartano Creative

Edited by Nan Allen Britt

ISBN: 1935827146

ISBN 13: 9781935827146

Atlanta, Georgia

DEDICATION

We would like to dedicate this book to...
Our ex-husbands who generously supplied us with
AFGEs.
And to our present husbands who are really good at
pointing out the mess before we step into it.

TABLE OF CONTENTS

FOREWORD

Charles L. Whitfield, MD

When I was in the middle of co-leading a therapy group for adult children of trauma in 1986, a group member was working on a particularly difficult conflict in her life. That was the first time I heard this term AFGE (Another F*ing Growth Experience). Her using that term got both a laugh and the attention of the group. As she worked on and through her emotional pain, it helped give an explanation and meaning to the possibility that we can use our upsets, difficulties and conflicts to grow. We can make lemonade out of lemons.

I have occasionally used this term in subsequent therapy groups and in a rare individual session. Naming it this way usually gets the person's attention more constructively and accurately on their particular upset. Naming an upset as being an AFGE helps us begin to "nail" it.

In this book Barbara and Sharon help us name and handle our conflicts and upsets in a clear and skilled way. They tell us how to identify, work through and eventually let go of our emotional pain and attachment to and worry about the AFGE.

In the process of healing from the effects of trauma and the big difficulties that may mount up in our lives, we usually go through multiple AFGEs in a seemingly never ending flow stretched over time. In 1987 I described this process in *Healing the Child Within*. Here is the diagram I used below showing each circle as an AFGE and the movement up if we learn from them.

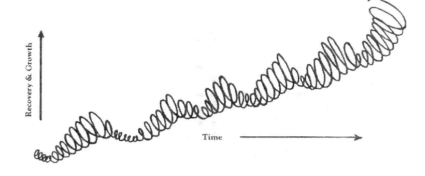

As Barbara and Sharon indicate throughout this book, if we name and work through them with our full conscious mental and emotional awareness, we can continue to grow with each AFGE.

In chapter 5, Barbara and Sharon address core issues in working through an AFGE. Of these, each AFGE nearly always involves the core issue of difficulty handling conflict. And any AFGE may involve any one or usually more of these core issues. The power of addressing core issues is that knowing about them helps us search for, name and finally work through and then let go of the emotional pain of our AFGE.

The beauty of this book lies in the spectrum of Barbara and Sharon's way of understanding and so clearly describing these bothersome upsets. Barbara addresses AFGEs from her long experience working through her own and assisting countless others in her group and individual therapy practice with me. Sharon comes from a Buddhist and yogic perspective which begins with knowing the Four Noble Truths of Buddhism that address attachment and suffering. I have watched their friendship and the blending of their wisdom over the years and admired their helping each other through countless AFGEs.

I've also noticed while watching them, that as soon as their problem is reframed as an AFGE, they begin to laugh, even moan, but in a lighter way that helps to move them through a conflict. This book will likely help you to do the same. Reframing our upset or drama by first naming it as an AFGE shifts our perspective and perception into a new and expansive dimension wherein we have more personal choices and power.

In this book Barbara and Sharon will show you the way.

Charles L. Whitfield, MD
Atlanta, GA 2012

N.B.: You may notice in Chapter 4 **ego vs. Soul** and throughout this book that the word "ego" is not capitalized. This is to remind us that the ego is "invented," in contrast to the Child Within/Soul/True Self which is real and so we capitalize them. The path that leads to peace and these real expressions of our Self is obstructed by the ego and in this respect, as Sharon and Barbara so beautifully explain, the ego needs to be tamed. This is perhaps one of the biggest roles of an AFGE, to help us to learn to let go of our ego.

INTRODUCTION

A "growth experience" is one you may either love to revisit in your memory or one you wish had never happened. It can be a moment of intense joy, a period of chaos and upheaval, or an achingly boring year in your life. However it manifests, it will likely teach and change us—if we are willing to look at it and learn from it.

We—Barbara and Sharon—have faced many such times and lived to tell the tale (and so will you), but it did take much courage coupled with a great deal of laughter. It also helps to have a friend along on this amazing journey called life. We have remained friends throughout these many years but took different paths on our journeys. In this book we will describe many different kinds of growth experiences from our two different views.

Part of this book will be more technical, giving facts, figures and dynamics about how and why we struggle in life, how to name those struggles so they lose some of their power over us, and then suggestions on how to work through them.

Barbara has spent many years in the recovery field with her husband Charles Whitfield, MD, a pioneer in a new field called "Trauma Psychology," which is directed toward helping people who were repeatedly traumatized as children. Barbara's insights on core and other issues in recovery come from her clinical experience in providing both individual and group psychotherapy to trauma survivors. Her spiritual writing comes from years of medical school research into the near-death experience and its aftereffects, plus her own spiritual experiences that guided her research.

Sharon has spent years studying and teaching the philosophies of yoga and Buddhism, as well as her take on the general psychology of how we live and survive in this modern world. Her "test kitchen" has been her life and experiences. In her workshops she helps students begin to find their own personal journey into attaining inner peace.

We have blended these two different yet ultimately similar and complimentary paths into what we know as one truth: *there are many paths, but they all lead to the same place if we trust in our own inner wisdom.* That place is where we find our True Self fully and totally healed, where we meet with the source of All— the serenity and completeness of Love.

We know that without the kick in the pants from our F*ing Growth Experiences neither of us would ever have had the courage to just laugh out loud at the ridiculousness of our self-important ego selves. The meek may inherit the earth, but those with a sense of humor usually have more fun and eventually inherit the joy and beauty of this earth and the life we are privileged to live.

Have fun reading this book, and in the rest of your life, learn, and when possible laugh, as you experience your own AFGEs. We both promise that if you do, AFGEs will lose their power over you, and you will gather that power where it belongs — in your own wonderful Self.

With love and peace,

Sharon and Barbara

PART 1

Awakening

CHAPTER 1

Defining AFGEs & Default Mode

Barbara: I gave two talks a few weeks ago that were challenging and at the same time a pleasure to finally present. The first one was at the Institute for the Study of Empathic Psychotherapy, Education and Living. The second was for the American Society of Addiction Medicine—two amazing and highly intellectual groups. My presentations were the only ones covering research into spirituality, and I called the talks "*Wisdom from the Light: Near-Death Research, Getting Real and the Power of the Hero's Journey.*"

Afterwards, I had a deep sense of gratitude for the opportunity to bring a talk on spirituality to these two organizations. This gratitude carried on for several days and then it hit -- my next challenging AFGE. I even called it my "Cosmic Koan."[1] I fell into a story of why I had to have something knock me down when I was feeling so high over these two accomplishments. I had been deeply betrayed by someone I had thought was my friend. I started wondering again if something bad has to happen every time something good happens. I was a wreck.

My friends surrounded me with their wisdom. I know how spiritually in tune they are and I respected what they told me, but it registered as advice and I wasn't ready yet to take it in. I was in my heart and it was hurting. I decided the best I could do was to let myself feel what was going on because continuing to get into a story about all this would just postpone feeling my feelings or what my husband Charlie and I advise to our psychotherapy group members—to get out of our head with its repetitive

---

1 **ko·an** *n*. A puzzling, often paradoxical statement or story, used in Zen Buddhism as an aid to meditation and a means of gaining spiritual awakening.

stories and watch the feelings move in and then eventually move out. Otherwise we get stuck in an avalanche of words.

So I hung out with the feelings for several days and the pain continued. There was nothing I could do. I was powerless over what someone else had done. I was so hurt and I hadn't even seen it coming.

One evening I was describing this painful process in my inner life to my husband Charlie and when I finished he said, "Well. It's just another AFGE!"

"It's a what?" I asked.

"Another AFGE! Another F*-ing Growth Experience."

I thought for a second that I had heard that several months ago and I started to laugh. I knew he was right. That is what I was in the middle of. (I had been quietly hoping all along that somehow I could grow from this hurt. That there would be a "pay off.")

And I was sitting with the feelings and waiting for the learning — the growth. That's why I was being so patient about it. I didn't have enough information and needed to sit with my feelings.

But wait! Now I was chuckling, (eventually I would be laughing) — for the first time since this unresolved problem, this emotional rollercoaster, this AFGE began. I was lightening up. I now had the beginnings of the bigger picture and it felt good. Within a few days I was trying on what my other friends had told me and their wisdom started to sink in.

With AFGEs *recognized* and *worked through* there is an advantage and reward at the end of its conflicted pain. The struggle gets smaller as soon as we can reframe it as an AFGE--Another F*-ing Growth Experience.

Sharon: It's all about the teachers. No, not your first or fourth grade teacher but the ones we meet every day, especially those people we really don't like. The know-it-all, the criticizer, the "I'm smarter than you" person. Those people that seem to make us crazy the minute they walk into our physical, mental or emotional space. Talk about knowing which of our buttons to push, these people seem to be "experts." But if we awaken to that, they can be our best teachers.

If we are aware, we will step back from the immediate emotional reaction they evoke in us and look deeply at what is really going on within our own mind and body. Why is this person's want, action or opinion of us so important? What long ago "button" are they pushing, and does it really apply to this moment, to where we are in our life now? With a little time, just like Barbara took in the above experience, we sit with the feelings and wait for the learning to come.

Often our initial negative reactions to people who are challenging us with their actions or words are reactions we had months or years ago to someone and something else. At the time the original situation happened we didn't or couldn't take the time to process what was going on, just as Barbara pointed out in her AFGE above.

Barbara is one of the wisest people I know. She has spent years as a counselor in private therapy practice with her husband, Charles Whitfield, MD and author of the seminal book *Healing the Child Within*. She is a respiratory therapist and wellness practitioner. Being recognized by the medical society for her deep knowledge and understanding of the spiritual aspect of medicine, she was asked to speak at two different but highly respected conferences. To be acknowledged as an expert in our chosen field is a wonderful accomplishment and one that Barbara deserved. So she was feeling full of gratitude and confidence, when Bam! It all changes — just as life always does. Another AFGE rears its ugly head. But Barbara stood still because she has learned to listen, to understand what is really happening is a growth experience. She knew she would learn something. She understands the gift of a good (or bad) teacher.

We have all heard the saying "What doesn't kill you makes you stronger." We do get stronger if we are willing to learn from the teacher in front of us. That teacher most often is someone or something telling us what we don't want to hear. That nasty cough that won't go away definitely isn't a smoker's cough even though we smoke a pack a day. Can't be that. Or the fight we had this morning with our wife/husband/friend. It wasn't our fault, it was their fault as usual. They just don't "understand" us, or even more irritating, they think they are right.

If there is something making us unhappy, angry, jealous or sad, more often than not it is coming from inside us. If we don't investigate our own inner life (see diagram below,) we aren't taking responsibility for our part, and that is usually because we don't want to take the time and energy to listen to the teaching. It is too much work. But if we don't do the work we will always be unhappy and dissatisfied. "Getting down on the floor and wrestling with it" describes the hard work of processing our feelings and whatever pain, sorrow or other painful emotions that come up. Acknowledging AFGEs and working through them is how we gain wisdom over time. Each processed and metabolized outcome collects and creates our wisdom as we also begin to understand just exactly who we are.

The results of working through life's AFGEs are a deeper sense of connection to our real self and others and the way to find contentment and happiness. This directly helps us reset our default mode. If we grew up without our needs being met, our original inner mood — what we refer to in this book as a "default mode" — is likely one of neediness and discomfort, fear and shame, or *whatever makes us discontent and unhappy*. If we grew up in a dysfunctional family, our default mode is probably not comfortable, and we may be so used to this feeling that we may not even notice that it's a struggle to feel "good."

—Beliefs —Needs —Thoughts
—Feelings —Wants —Decisions

—Choices   —Experiences
—Dreams —Creativity —Fantasies
—Sensations   —Intuitions

—Higher Self   —Primal feelings
—Unconscious experiences
—Insights and revelations

—Higher sense perceptions
—Unfinished business
—Connection to God

My Inner Life—It is important to become fully aware of what is coming up for us from moment to moment in our inner life, to observe our own heart and mind at work.

Default Mode

Our most common definition of default is a preset option as in computer technology. We have observed that we also have a default mode in our inner life. By that we mean that the mood or mindset that we revert to goes back to early child development. So, for an example, when we are stressed we automatically go back to the mindset we had as children in the way we were taught to handle stress. Our default setting can manifest in other situations too.

Barbara: I have had the joy of taking care of our little granddaughter, Lily, for over four years. I started doing that when she was six weeks old and her mother went back to work. I thought I would care for her until she was six months so she could get a good start without being exposed to other babies and their illnesses. At six months, I knew there was no way anyone was taking care of this child but me.

She comes to Charlie and me every day, Monday through Friday, with a smile on her face and an open heart. Her default is peace and joy. She spontaneously sings while playing by herself. Things may come up that upset her occasionally, but within a few moments she reverts back to her default mode.

Sharon: Recently, my son, Brian and his fiancée, Ashley, got married on the beach in Florida. Kaia, Ashley's 8-year-old daughter, spent the weekend skipping around, smiling with pure abandon and joy. Barbara and I loved the fact that her default mode was always joyful.

These two young girls have been given everything they need to carry them through life with a foundation of security, love, recognition, trust in themselves and their place in the world. They are treated with a sense of respect and self-worth. Their parents also give them a sense of healthy boundaries when appropriate.

How different this is from the kind of childhood many of us experienced.

Barbara: Until doing the inner work necessary, my default mode had always been scanning my surroundings to determine if I was safe—a need to feel secure. So I always felt anxiety, which is a current code word for fear. Coming from a severely dysfunctional family was stressful enough. As an adult I continued to carry that stress in my inner life.

Sharon: My default mode has always been an underlying sense of peacefulness. My mother trusted the world around her, so she trusted in my safety. When I was a child I was allowed to go outside and explore. I went to the little stream in the woods behind my house and sat by the water just observing the birds and other small creatures that moved around me. I didn't see myself separate from nature. I still don't. That early default mode helped me create and keep a source of inner peacefulness even though parts of my childhood were very difficult.

The purpose of this book, the purpose of using AFGEs to grow, is to reset a default mode that doesn't work for you.

We can reframe these AFGE experiences as being lessons we can use to contribute to our psychological and spiritual growth. To "get through" them without having the awareness of a deeper underlying learning experience or "lesson" would be to waste them and slow our own personal growth. By reframing our problems and dilemmas as AFGEs, we 1) move away from the story that keeps getting bigger as our ego/false self continues to spin, and 2) gain a healthier sense of humor and/or serenity with an eventual possible payoff. (Note: Not all AFGEs have "happy endings." Sometimes, we just have to let go and trust that it will work out to our benefit, whatever that may be. And that in itself creates more wisdom.)

Default Outlook

Those who were fortunate to have a happy childhood with loving parents and harmony from their sibs, will likely have a "default" (a mental state they revert to naturally) that is peaceful and happier. The rest of us may unfortunately have a default that is painful. It could be fear, mistrust, anger, sadness, negativity, etc. We need to "reset" our default mode, and AFGEs are an effective way to reset.

Whatever our default is, don't believe that it is permanent. There's always a reset button and we will show you how to use it.

We have the power to change painful or uncomfortable background noise in our inner life to a default mode of contentment by working through AFGEs and watching ourselves become more than we ever thought we could be. We become who we were meant to be– peaceful, wise, and loving human beings who can experience joy when it comes up, instead of running from it because we aren't used to it.

Your Default Mode

Spend a few moments now remembering what it was like for you as a young child.

Does your default mode need adjusting? Do you need to move out of a setting that doesn't serve you or won't let you be your real self?

We have a choice. We don't need to be unhappy, anxious, depressed or sad anymore. With our Higher Power or our inner wisdom, we are the co-creator of us.

We are offering you all of the tools that we have used, and you can apply them to yourself. Take what works for you and leave the rest. Then, welcome to our world where joy and happiness is the default mode.

KEY CONCEPTS RELATED TO AFGES

	Barbara	Sharon
Key Terms	*Taken from Trauma Psychology and The Study of Near-Death Experiences*	*A blending of Buddhist Psychology concepts, yogic philosophy and energy healing*
AFGE	Another F*ing Growth Experience. When it comes, at first it appears to be out of our control. What we do with it is in our control. It can be a gift in disguise.	An AFGE is a way to actively seek and engage our problems in order to understand them.
Default Mode	The mood, painful response and attitude we revert to naturally. Paying attention to our AFGEs helps to reset our emotional pain to a more pleasant, peaceful, even joyful mood.	Our habitual state of mind. This state can be negative or positive. AFGEs help us change negative states to positive ones. We use our problems to solve our problems.

	Barbara	Sharon
ego	False self. An assistant we think we need to help us survive. A good slave, a horrible master. A belief about ourselves that we are separated from others and God and are completely on our own.	Our personal concept of our individual self. This self is deeply affected by our past traumas
Unconscious responses	Reacting from our ego	Reacting instead of responding with awareness.
Waking up	Using AFGEs to recognize and understand reactions from our old wounds and our egos so we can become more conscious.	Understanding that our thoughts create our world. Change our thoughts and we change our world.
Conscious responses	Acting from our common sense and intuition. Comes from the wisdom gained from AFGEs. Also called being in the Now or being awake.	Letting go of habitual negative patterns and relating to life from a positive, loving inner self. Knowing and living to our full potential.

	Barbara	Sharon
Core Issues	An issue is any conflict, concern or potential problem, whether conscious or unconscious, that is incomplete for us or needs action or change. A core issue is one that comes up repeatedly.	Attachment to things that are pleasant and aversion to those that are unpleasant and not recognizing these patterns as we continually repeat them
Humility	The openness and willingness to learn more about self, others and the God of our Understanding	Surrendering the ego in order to feel our connection to others and the universe.
Soul	Our True Self that is ultimately eternal.	Our True Self that is ultimately eternal
Spirituality	A vast experience that ultimately involves a direct connection to a Higher Power	A long walk toward and inward to your Soul

GENERAL DEFINITIONS

Awareness: Observation of our thoughts and emotions in an AFGE and using that knowledge to affect change for the positive.

Mindfulness: To be present in the moment, especially in an AFGE, to learn our habitual thought patterns and cultivate ways of changing those patterns.

Trauma Psychology: Trauma psychology focuses on the wounds and pain we have suffered in our past, such as a dysfunctional family environment; abusive parents; addiction or alcohol abuse, etc. through individualized therapy seeking to bring about understanding, healing and growth.

Buddhist Psychology: Recognizes suffering as universal, that all of us suffer and that our thoughts perpetuate our problems. Studying our AFGEs (problems) we can learn to stop our destructive thoughts and patterns and realize our full potential, our True Self.

Using both these forms of psychology within the framework of dealing with our AFGEs helps us solve our problems and cultivate a stronger, clearer and healthier inner spirit.

Meditation: Any length of time set aside for quiet and internal contemplation. A period of resting the mind, to be truly aware of our thoughts and how our mind works.

CHAPTER 2

Our Near-Death Experiences as The "Ultimate Teaching Tool" [2]

Barbara: My near-death experience occurred 37 years ago while I was in the hospital recuperating from surgery. About two days after surgery, complications set in and I started to die. I remember waking up in a circle bed and seeing my huge belly. I had swollen up, and the swelling was pulling my incisions open and it hurt. I called for my nurse and started screaming.

People in white came rushing in. It was a dramatic scene, just like those you see in hospital dramas on television. I had no idea what was going on because I was not a respiratory therapist yet. It seemed like everybody was pushing carts and machinery, throwing things back and forth over me. They hooked me up to all kinds of machinery, tubes, monitors and bags.

Overwhelmed emotionally, I lost consciousness and later that night woke up in the hall outside my room. I floated back into the room and saw my body. I felt peaceful, more peaceful than I had ever been in this lifetime. Then I went into a tunnel where I was greeted and held by my grandmother who had been dead for 14 years. Before this I had never once thought about her surviving her death. I didn't believe in that. But now I knew I was with her. Her love enveloped me and together we relived all our memories of each other. I could see and feel all this not only from my own mental and emotional perspective but from hers too. And I know she experienced how her actions and her love had comforted me in my childhood.

---

2 Ring K *Lessons From the Light.* Barbara's friend and colleague, Kenneth Ring, coined the terms: "Ultimate Teaching Tool" and "Cosmic Equalizer" after interviewing hundreds of near-death experiencers.

Suddenly I was back in my body, back in the circle bed. Two nurses were opening my drapes. The sunlight was startling. It hurt my eyes so I asked them to close the drapes. I tried to tell my nurses and then several doctors that I had left the bed. They told me that it was impossible and that I had been hallucinating.

My Life Review

About a week later, I again left my body in the circle bed. I was no longer on the critical list, but I was still debilitated and weak. I had been rotated forward onto my face. I was uncomfortable. I seemed to have been in that position for too long. I reached for the call button, but it had slipped away from where it had been clipped to the bed sheet. I started to call, then yell, then scream frantically, but my door was closed. When no one came I became hysterical. Then I separated from my body.

As I left my body, I again went out into the darkness, only this time I was awake and could see it happening. Looking down and off to the right, I saw myself in a bubble—in the circle bed—crying. Then I looked up to the left and I saw my one-year-old self in another bubble—face down in my crib—crying just as hard. I looked to the right and saw myself again in the circle bed, then to the left and saw myself as a baby. I looked back and forth about three more times.

Then I let go. I decided I did not want to be the thirty-two-year-old Barbara anymore; I'd go to the baby. As I moved away from my body in the circle bed, I felt as though I had released myself from this lifetime. As I did, I became aware of an Energy that was wrapping itself around me and going through me, permeating me, holding up every molecule of my being.

Even though I had been an atheist for years, I felt God's love. This love was holding me. It felt incredible. There are no words in the English language, or maybe in this reality, to explain the kind of love God emanates. God was *totally accepting* of everything we—God and I— reviewed in my life.

In every scene of my life review I could feel again what I had felt at various times in my life. And I could feel *everything* that everyone else had felt as a consequence of my presence and my actions. Some of it felt good and some of it felt awful. All of this translated into knowledge, *and I learned. Oh, how I learned!*

The information was flowing at such an incredible speed that it probably would have burned me up if it hadn't been for the extraordinary loving Energy that was holding me. The information came in, and then God's Love neutralized my judgments against myself. In other words, throughout every scene I viewed, information flowed through me about my perceptions and feelings, and the perceptions and feelings of every person who had shared those scenes with me. No matter how I judged myself in each interaction, being held by God was the bigger interaction. God interjected God's Love into everything, every feeling, every bit of information about absolutely everything that went on, so that everything was all right. There was no good and no bad. There was only me— and my loved ones from this life— trying to survive, just trying to *be.*

I realize now that without God holding me, I would not have had the strength to experience what I did.

When it started, God and I were merging. We became one, so that I could see through God's eyes and feel through God's heart. Together, we witnessed how severely I had treated myself because that was the behavior shown and taught to me as a child. I realized that the only big mistake I had made in my thirty-two years of life was that I had never learned to love myself.

God let me into God's experience of all this. I felt God's memories of these scenes through God's eyes. I could sense God's divine intelligence, and it was astonishing. God loves us and wants us to wake up to our real selves, to what is important. I realized that God wants us to know that *we only experience real pain if we die without living first.* And the way to live is to give love to others *and* to ourselves. It seems that we are here to learn to give and receive love. But only when we heal enough to be real can we understand and give and receive love the way love was meant to be.

When God holds us and we merge into One, we remember this feeling as being limitless. God is limitless. God's capacity to love is never-ending. God's love for us never changes, no matter who and how we are. God doesn't judge us. We judge ourselves by *feeling* the love we have created in other's lives. We also feel the pain we have caused in other's lives. This may be a kind of "Cosmic Equalizer."[3]

I did not see an old man with a white beard who sits on a throne in judgment of us. I felt only limitless divine love.

God only gives. God interjected love into all the scenes of my life to show me God's reality. And the most amazing part of all is that God held nothing back. I understood all that God understood. God let me in. God shared all of God's Self with me: all the qualities of gentleness and openness, and all the gifts, including our own empowerment and peace. I never knew that much loving intelligence and freedom could exist.

What I Saw In My Life Review

At this point God and I were merging into one Sacred Person. It felt as though I lifted off the circle bed as we went to the baby I was seeing to my upper left in the darkness. Picture the baby being in a bubble; that bubble was in the center of a cloud of thousands and thousands of bubbles. In each bubble was another scene from my life. As we moved toward the baby (infant me), it was as though we were bobbing through the bubbles. At the same time, there was a linear sequence in which we relived thirty-two years of my life. I could hear myself saying, "No wonder, no wonder." I now believe my "no wonders" meant "No wonder you are the way you are now. Look what was done to you when you were a little girl."

---

3 Ring K Personal communication

As my life unfolded, I witnessed how severely I had treated myself because that was the behavior shown and taught to me as a child. I realized that the only big mistake I had made in my life was that I had never learned to love myself. And I also realized that I was being given the gift of learning the whole truth— not the scattered fractured memories I had of my childhood— but the whole truth with the guidance to learn how to go beyond my wounds and heal.

And then I was back here, in this reality.

Sharon's Near-Death Experience

When I was 23, I was hospitalized for a routine appendectomy, underwent the surgery and was recovering in my room. I fell asleep and had a vivid dream with a voice calling my name, telling me I had to wake up, to Wake Up! I woke up and turned to the woman in the next bed, asking her to call a doctor, because I felt "funny." The next thing I knew I was falling backward, but I never felt the bed under me. Instead I found myself high up in the corner of the room, looking down at myself on the bed. My thought was: "If I'm not there, on the bed, where am I?"

I looked upward and the whole room disappeared, just softly fell away, and I was in the universe. That is the only way I can describe it... the universe. All around me was warm, soft light. I felt as though I had been here before or that this was where I should be. I wasn't afraid – just curious. I seemed to be able to move (it was more like floating) forward, and as I did so I sensed the presence of my mother, who had died after a short illness, when I was sixteen. When my mother died there had been no time to talk with her, to share words of love and goodbye and now, here in this place, she was all around me. There was a complete filling up within me of her love. I wasn't seeing her in the conventional sense of "seeing," but I was sensing her. Having lost her physical presence in my life when I was sixteen, feeling her now was beautiful. There was a soft wrapping of love around me and through me, my mother's love finally finding me again and gently holding me. I was one with her. There was no separation. The deep wound in my heart was healed and the ache of her absence subsided, then disappeared. I experienced immense joy. It is hard to find words that explain this experience. I'm trying to give some idea of what it felt like and where I was. How it felt to be so completely perfect.

Without any awareness of it happening, my mother moved softly on, and I was again in the warm, soft light. Here I asked the questions: Where am I? What is life? What about good and evil? I remember thinking: "Oh, yes, of course. I knew that." I was getting answers but there were no words. There was a deep understanding within me of all that was. Was this God? It felt like so much more. But whatever It was brought me a deep peace and understanding that quieted my questions and left me whole.

I gently "floated" toward what seemed to be a place or maybe a person... it was vague... but it was my destination. And I was filled with such a spacious joy to be finally there wherever "there" was. I was complete.

But as I have learned so often in life, it was not to be, not at this time. I felt my Self being pulled back with a strong hard jerk, and I literally slammed back into my body. I felt the jolt physically. It hurt. It hurt deep in my heart because I did not want to be here, back in my body. I wanted to be There.

I opened my eyes to see a doctor looming over me, pressing down on my chest. Two nurses were holding up the bottom of the bed. I was crying as the doctor gently leaned forward and told me it would be okay. I couldn't talk. I couldn't tell him of my despair, that I didn't want to be back. But then, ever so gently, a whisper reached me. A whisper that said: "This is where you are meant to be. Everything is all right." I understood and was comforted. My life would never be the same.

The first change is that I have no fear of death. Most people who have had NDE's don't fear death because we have seen something of what happens after death. We have experienced its wonderful mystery, full of joy and anticipation. There is no hell or purgatory. It can be called any number of things: heaven, paradise, Brahman, God, the Source, and all cultures have some sort of description, but my belief is that it is the purest form of love. It is made of the energy of love that we create as we live, and this energy extends beyond our bodies and minds. It joins with other sources of love energy that exist in what quantum physics describes as the non-local realm of vibrating energy where everything and everyone exists in a complex net of interdependent relationships. This net of energy is constantly exchanging information and is constantly changing. It is the area of ultimate possibility. Quantum physics is complex and I don't pretend to understand it fully, but I do believe that everyone is connected on a deep level and feel certain that one day it will be proven to be so. This was the greatest of the gifts from my NDE: the knowledge that Love is really all there is and all we need.

A near death experience is the ultimate growth experience.

CHAPTER 3

What happens after a Near-Death Experience?

Barbara: Looking at the research into the aftereffects of the near-death experience, we get an even deeper look at why some people welcome AFGEs for their own growth and release from painful thinking. Here is a list compiled by Bruce Greyson, MD:

Decreased fear of dying
A greater appreciation for life
Self-acceptance
Heightened sense of purpose
Greater self-understanding
Desire to learn
Elevated Spirituality (not more religious)
Greater Ecological and Planetary Concern
Heightened Intuition, empathy, compassion
Greater Concern and Empathy for Others
Increased Physical and Psychic Sensitivity
Higher Sensitivity to Light and Sound
Higher Sensitivity to Alcohol and Other Drugs

If we take these traits and cluster them, this is what people are drawn to:

Self-actualization, Altruism, and
Natural Spirituality.

This is an impressive list of reasons to open our inner life to AFGEs with an attitude of "Bring 'em on" and facing them with a sense of humor since there will be something positive happening in the process.

Now here's the good news for those of you who don't want to nearly die to get a transformative experience. There are many other ways to embrace these aftereffects listed above. My audiences have been informing me about other ways or what we call "triggers" for over 30 years now. This is the list I compiled: [4] Mark any that may apply to you.

Near-Death

Childbirth

Meditation

Intense Prayer

Death of a loved one

Detox from alcohol or other drugs

Overwhelming loss

Transcendental sexual experience

Spontaneously (No trigger. It just happens!)

Spiritual literature or hearing a Spiritual talk

Some Psychedelic Drug Experiences

Working a 12 Step Program

Hearing a Spiritual talk

A "Big Dream" (One that is never forgotten and create all of the same positive aftereffects)

---

4 There is now an organization that reports on these other triggers and certifies therapists to assist people to process them in therapy. It's called "ACISTE" The American Center for the Integration of Spiritually Transformative Experiences (www.aciste.org).

Kundalini Experience[5]

Yoga/Meditation Experience

Breath and Body work

Trauma/Transcendence Interface [6]

Synchronicities

And, the one we wish we could have had (instead of nearly dying):

Reading about NDEs, or hearing someone tell theirs.

That's right! What you the reader are doing right now.

The aftereffects are contagious. The researchers who have studied these experiences have validated the fact that they are changed by them just as much as the experiencers. And, they've even polled interested people who have read the books and heard the talks — they are changed too.

Sharon: After my NDE I began to search in earnest to understand just what is this being we call God, and did the religious explanation of God match what I had experienced. I found there were many sources that said their definition of God was the only one and that you had to follow their rules. But that was not what I had felt and experienced. In fact, it was the complete opposite of all that, the near death experience brought about a new dimension. What I had felt in death was that it was important to live this life fully and to live it with deep love and compassion.

So I continued to study and read religious texts and philosophies from the Bible, the Koran, the Nag Hammadi as well as Kant, Sartre, and Socrates to name a few. I read and read, sure that at

---

5 Whitfield B (1995) Spiritual Awakenings
6 Lehmann A, Doctoral Dissertation, personal communication.

least one of them would come close to my near-death experience and what my heart told me was real.

Buddhism came the closest with the teaching of the Brahma-Viharas also known as the practice of loving-kindness. It gave me a foundation for understanding what I had felt. I had been in and would one day return to the perfect, complete manifestation of loving-kindness.

The aftereffects of an NDE continue to impact me, and one of those impacts is the ability to sense when I am in the middle of a life situation that will have some lessons to teach me. That doesn't necessarily mean I will love the lesson I have to learn. By now you are probably beginning to understand that an AFGE is usually stressful and not fun. It is human to want only pleasant experiences, to try and avoid unpleasantness whenever it shows up. The tough AFGE's help us realize how to approach life with an attitude of learning so we can ultimately live a deeper more meaningful life. Through understanding an AFGE we can learn how to let go of old patterns and habits that keep us from being happy and content. We can use the AFGE experiences to transform and transcend old hurts, to leap forward with eagerness into life.

My NDE was an incredible AFGE. Rather than feeling that I was caught in what life had "dealt" me, I used this experience to trust that I had it in me to live to my full potential, to be my best self.

You also have that power. All you need to do is look inside, to see the deep Source of wisdom that you already own and refuse to listen to the Greek Chorus of negative voices that constantly tell you that your efforts are not good enough and that you are not good enough-just let them go. Stop listening and start transforming.

CHAPTER 4

ego vs. Soul

Barbara: So often I hear my patients asking, "Why?"

When life is interrupted by events out of our control, I hear myself asking the same thing. These events sometimes knock us down so violently that we have to pick ourselves up, brush ourselves off and start all over again. As we wrote about earlier, we gain some clarity by calling these events AFGEs. Now, we will take this a step further by looking at who's in charge of us when we get caught up. Is it our ego or our Soul?

Here's a poem I wrote that I reread every time I am questioning who's in charge of my inner life:

Flipping

The ego suffers
By resisting pain.
The Soul learns
By metabolizing it.

The ego believes
It will die.
The Soul knows
It returns to Eternal Reality.

The ego ages in linear time.
The Soul becomes radiant-
And wise.

The ego is isolated and feels alone.
The Soul knows it is part
Of something much Bigger.

The ego lives stressed.
The Soul relaxes into life.

The ego is addicted to drama
To grow more of itself.
The Soul lives with peace of mind.

The ego may know that enlightenment
Is not real but keeps trying to grasp it.
The Soul knows that a new enlightenment
Comes with each lesson
Of each problem that life brings us.

The ego suffers.
The Soul celebrates.

ego and Soul have one thing in common:
When they are in action
They grow more of themselves.
It's our choice
Every single time.

Barbara: Our ego sustains itself by collecting conflicts and resentments to strengthen its hold on us. Our ego needs conflict to stay strong. Working through various AFGEs over time, I learned to disengage from my ego and transcend to a peaceful existence where my ego couldn't go. In that "peaceful place," my ego couldn't trick me into identifying with it if I was confronted with a relationship that was begging to pull me into a painful experience. (However, as I said in the introduction to this book, I still get caught in it occasionally. Hopefully, I'm catching on faster and watching my recovery time become shorter as I practice with the same tools we are sharing in this book.)

In fact, the AFGE method is working so well (and all the other tools that come along to help us when we move into the Soul's flow of Spiritual growth and recovery) I have actually watched my relationships with myself, Charlie, our adult kids, others and God transcend to a place I have longed for since my near-death experience 37 years ago. This place is free of the drama that surrounds conflict, or if there is drama, the people I love are as aware of it as I am and we try to co-commit to step out of the drama and find a neutral zone where it's not **either/or** but **both/ and.** We **both** have our valid points **and** let's move on! [7]

Many near-death experiencers at one time or another, long to go back to where they went in their NDE. But I have learned as I've worked on myself and counseled other NDErs, that what we want to recapture is not that place we were in, but who we were when we died — pure Soul. And we can be pure Soul here and now. This means living an authentic life from the deepest part of our Soul, or as some people explain — living from our "hearts."

ego

Our ego suffers because it resists pain. Our Soul takes in what is happening in a way that allows for pain to help us learn and move through it. Our ego freezes in a depressed state. Our Soul understands how to move through pain, which then transforms into a bittersweet renewal. The table below demonstrates the difference between our ego and our Soul both in our internal dialogue (inner life) and our outer dialogue with others.

ego can be positive or negative. When the ego is helpful to us, such as in screening, sorting and handling many aspects of our internal and external reality, we can call it positive ego. My positive ego is writing this. Your positive ego is reading it. Positive ego balances our checkbook, keeps us on time for appointments, etc. When it tries to take over and control our life, however, it becomes negative ego, also known as false self or co-dependent self. This part of us believes we are annihilated when we die. It may believe in the Universe as an intellectual head trip. And it often believes it is a victim.

---

7 Whitfield C, Whitfield B, Prevatt J, Park R (2006)*The Power of Humility: Choosing Peace over Conflict in Relationships.* Health Communications, Inc. Deerfield Beach, FL More from this book in Chapter 7.

TABLE OF EGO VS. SOUL

ego traits	Soul Traits
Flatters	Informs
Commands	Suggests
Demands	Guides
Tests	Nudges
Chooses for you	Leaves choice to you
Imprisons	Empowers
Promotes dependence	Promotes independence
Intrudes	Respects
Pushes	Supports
Excludes	Includes
Instills fear	Promotes well-being
Becomes bored easily; not at peace	Realizes peace when doing nothing
Is status oriented	Is free and open
Judges	Accepts Individuality
Demands obedience	Encourages growth and development
Implies having ultimate authority	Recognizes a Higher Power
Offers shortcuts	Offers integration
Seeks personal gratification	Extends Unconditional Love
Self-righteous	Humility
Suffers while resisting what is	Feels the pain and lets it go.

© Barbara Whitfield 2009

An easy way to tell if you are in your ego or being your True Self is to wait until you are doing nothing. As you relax into "doing nothing," are you feeling bored? Or is there a quiet feeling of peaceful *being* deep within you? If you are bored, it's likely your ego complaining. If you are peaceful, this is your True Self just "being." When I realize I feel bored, I try saying a spontaneous prayer of gratitude. My heart/Soul may scan all I am grateful for and this may bring me back to a state of peaceful being.

Sharon: As we look at the difference between ego and Soul we also need to realize that our ego is not all bad. As Barbara states above, we have positive ego and negative ego traits. After all it is how we relate to the world around us, it is a part of our individual identity at work and in our relationships. But often we lose sight of the fact that ego is not who we truly are, it is only the outward aspect of us. The real, true us resides in our heart, which is another word for Soul. For instance, Barbara and I are from the same Soul Space but we traveled different paths throughout our lives. Barbara's path took her from research into NDE's to taking that knowledge into providing therapy and counseling for those in recovery from myriad types of trauma and addiction. My path followed the spiritual call of the East and I found Buddhism to resonate with my deeper True Self and then took that into the teaching of yoga, meditation and mindfulness.

Both of our paths required that we investigate how our ego and Soul were heard. All paths, philosophies and religions ask us to commit to finding our Soul and *keeping our ego* healthy but *not in charge*. AFGEs are one of our Soul's ways of getting our attention, and usually we will find that ego has instigated parts if not all of an AFGE.

So how do we begin to work with an AFGE when it happens? I think the first thing we need to do is just stop — stop negative, circuitous thinking and step back. Most AFGEs are based in a fear of some sort. It could be fear of abandonment by someone we love, fear of losing financial stability, or fear that we will be alone. Whatever it is, our ego will be there trying to keep us worked up and fighting, to keep the status quo because ego is afraid of change. But the fact is that life is all about change. Nothing ever stays the same, not people, not places. Think back ten years, are you the same person now? Of course not. You have learned new things, grown older and hopefully wiser, but one thing is definitely sure — you have changed. The positive take on this is that change is your best friend for it allows you to get in touch with who you really are, and AFGEs help us move out of ignorance and into the true wisdom of our self.

But if we release ego's hold and understand that what we really need is a basic understanding of the core issue involved we can better understand what we need to do. (Core issues will be discussed in the next chapter.) Referring to the table above, we can see what ego traits are being triggered in the AFGE and then look to which Soul Traits we could incorporate to help us move through the AFGE. The greatest teacher is our own real inner self and the ability to learn from our mistakes and not make them again. In doing this we rid ourselves of ignorance, and what Buddhists call unskillful actions.

Both Buddhism and yoga encourage us to explore our inner world to discover what we are afraid of. Bringing our dark fears forward we shine the light of understanding on them so they disappear like so much smoke. But first we need to identify those fears, those often terrifying, deep-seated Core Issues.

So now we can step back from our problem and give it a name, AFGE, hoping that this may give us at least a little chuckle and distance from "our story." Next, as we just learned, we begin to understand who's in charge of our inner life. Are we going to continue to let our ego spin more pain about our story? Or can we settle into our Soul so our real self or heart can run this show?

CHAPTER 5

Core Issues and AFGEs

Barbara: In trauma and Twelve Step Recovery we talk about "Core Issues." Most growth experiences and AFGEs are connected to one or many of our personal core issues.

My husband Charles is a medical doctor who specializes in helping people recover from addictions, compulsions, or growing up in a dysfunctional family. He has written extensively on these topics, and in his most recent book, *The Wisdom to Know the Difference,*[8] the entire focus is on the fifteen core issues that people develop as ego defenses to protect themselves from feeling psychological pain. The value in knowing what these core issues are is that we can become more conscious of what we are actually experiencing. As we gain awareness we become more empowered to live as our True Selves (also called Soul, or our Child Within) rather than as our false, codependent self (sometimes called our negative ego). Learning about core issues and naming them when they become part of our response to whatever AFGE we're facing is a major aid in becoming a psychologically healthy person.

These are the 15 core issues:

- Difficulty resolving conflict
- Feelings
- Control
- Trust
- Being real
- Low self-esteem / shame
- Dependence
- Fear of abandonment

---

8 Whitfield C (2012) *Wisdom to Know the Difference: Core Issues in Relationships, Recovery and Living.* Muse House Press, Atlanta, GA

- All-or-none thinking and behaving
- High tolerance for inappropriate behavior
- Over-responsibility for others
- Neglecting my own needs
- Grieving my ungrieved hurts, losses and traumas
- Difficulty giving love, and difficulty receiving love

Listed below are short descriptions to begin to help us to recognize these core issues because *once we know we are in an AFGE*, we can switch our attention to the core issue and move out of the drama and into the healing work:

Difficulty resolving conflict

This is at the top of the AFGE chart. Life hands us conflicts. It's part of being human. I'm still not sure I can "handle" them but I now know I can "endure" them. Conflicts used to cause me to feel like the wicked witch melting at the end of *The Wizard of Oz*! Because conflicts are natural to being alive, we need to see them as AFGEs and practice getting through them without melting. [9]

Feelings

Research has shown that if we stick with a feeling and don't "cloak" it in a verbal story, it will come and go in 90 seconds. If, however, we remain angry after those 90 seconds have passed,

---

9 And by the way, if you didn't see the wonderful Broadway play *Wicked*, then you don't know that the wicked witch wasn't really wicked. She had experienced one AFGE after another from the day she was born. She was born with a green complexion, and it went downhill from there. In this new play the witch handled all this with great integrity and was actually a noble person who kept her humility and integrity during multiple AFGEs. She was a perfectly beautiful example of living from our Soul.

then it is because we have chosen to let that circuit in our brain continue to run. [10]

If my anger goes on much longer, or what I call "ad nauseam" it's time to name it as an AFGE so I can learn how to get out and stay out. I visualize the hamster running on the wheel. (And of course, in my AFGEs the hamster is me). If I am running on anger, it's time to do some anger bat work (Yes. We have one. We keep it in our group room for use in our therapy groups. I use it when I decide it may help with an upset because it feels good to get the anger out physically.) If you don't have an anger bat, hit a pillow or a towel will do. Think about what you are feeling and wring a dry towel. Face towels are a good size. Really get into the feeling as you zero in on getting that towel as wrung as possible.

Screaming in the car (with the windows rolled up and no one else with you) works well too. I try to wait for a red light to do it. Eventually, when we allow all the uncomfortable feelings to move through us, the joyful feelings are easier to feel and our feelings are fun. We just have to remember to not "numb out" to our feelings or here comes another AFGE.

Control

I was having some trouble giving up the urge of wanting to control a painful situation with one of my adult children. Then I had this dream. I was coming down the elevator from a top floor of an apartment house. As I walked through the lobby a woman on a phone in a booth (are you old enough to remember phone booths?) looked out and said to me, "Relax. This whole area is safe!" And I felt my dream self relax. I walked out to my car (not really. It was a huge SUV.) and I tried to get in the driver's side which was locked. I walked around to the passenger side and it was open. I realized I didn't have my purse and was going to go back inside and up the elevator to get it. A voice in my dream self's head told me that I didn't need my purse anymore (could

10 Jill Bolte Taylor *My Stroke of Insight* p.146 Penguin USA

that mean my identity? I had been studying the Eastern concept of "Being Nobody Special" and loved it. It released me from a lot of inner life spin.) Then the voice told me to relax and get used to being the passenger while "It" drove me around — from now on. I was pretty sure that voice was my (our) Higher Power.

I was grateful for that dream and I released my son to [hopefully] his highest good.

Trust

Oh Boy! I could write a whole book on the core issue of trust. Having grown up in a severely dysfunctional home, trust has always been my biggest core issue, or so it seems in my inner life. The first half of my life I handled trust by not handling it. I gave it away to everyone else. Ouch! Looking back now, well—at least I am at the point where I can chuckle. Some AFGE's are a string that lasts for years until we start to wake up and become aware of them. So I became aware of how I trusted everyone else, and then I started to do the exact opposite, I didn't trust anyone! Now, when this issue raises it's "Ugly Head" [I picture it as a snake coming out of a basket], I immediately label it as a possible AFGE and ask myself if I'm seeing clearly, or do I need to consult with someone else who is waking up too.

All-or-none thinking and behaving

What I just described in the core issue above, trust, is all-or-none thinking. Either I trusted everyone, or I trusted no one.

This is an interesting core issue because it's impractical to ever think we can have it all. So what's left — NOTHING! Watch the way you say things and how you behave. If everything is black and white, either/or, and mostly negative, then your AFGEs are high drama caused by all-or-none thinking and behaving.

Being Real

Here's how I handle this one:

A significant person in my life telling me to "stop being *that way!*"

Here's an AFGE being born. I try to nip it in the bud! First, I ask myself, "Is *'that way'* comfortable for me? Is this what I have chosen and/or is it serving my highest good?"

I also know that my close others aren't trying to hurt me. They are just being the perfect "edition" of who they are right now. So *I decide if I am being real,* and if I am, then I make sure I have a healthy boundary between them and me. I visualize this by keeping what is them on their side of the boundary and what is me on my side. This way I don't take on their "stuff" and the AFGE is avoided. If I slip up and take their opinion on, then I'm often in another AFGE. It gets easier as time goes on with practice for these "Being Real AFGEs."

When I start to feel uncomfortable from feeling like I have just "given myself away," I name it as an AFGE. I realize that my core issue is Being Real, and I take myself back! [Sorry guys! Maybe it's your turn to work on an AFGE! (and sadly, I'm the last one that can tell them that!)]

Low Self-Esteem or Shame

Nobody else better try this one on me. I used to do a good job on myself and now if I or anyone else tries this one on me — Watch out, big time AFGE!

Low Self-Esteem (code word "Shame") is endemic to we who grew up in dysfunctional homes. It drains all our energy internally and takes all the joy out of life. When we feel it — immediately call it an AFGE and "just say 'NO!'"

Dependence

We live in a world with others all around us, and it's normal to have some dependence and independence. The balanced way here is also to have some interdependence on each other without our real self disappearing. If you feel too dependent go back up to "Being Real" and start from there. If we're too dependent our significant other is going to hand us lots of AFGEs .

Fear of abandonment

Fearing abandonment because we will feel lonely is an AFGE.

Enjoying being alone is not.

When we stop fearing abandonment, we enjoy being with ourselves.

And the pay off when we stop fearing and enjoy being alone is -- people can feel that enjoyment in us and want to be around us.

High tolerance for inappropriate behavior

If we grew up in a dysfunctional family we have high tolerance for inappropriate behavior. We needed to learn to do this to survive. Looking around at our culture, we are also showing high tolerance for inappropriate behavior in our compulsion to be *politically correct,* which has too often stifled our real self and our creativity. As adults we don't need to hang on to codependent relationships anymore to survive. We can develop "low tolerance" for inappropriate behavior and free ourselves of constant drama.

Over-responsibility for others

If we had to take care of our parents, instead of our parents taking care of us so we could have a healthy fun childhood — then we learned to be overly responsible for others and we may not even know we are doing it. But reading this book about AFGEs hopefully makes us more aware of what is draining us. This is a big revelation when we first figure it out. We all need to take care of ourselves and if our over-responsibility is stopping us from becoming independent, we need to step back. What a relief!

Neglecting my own needs

This goes with the one above. (Actually, they are all intertwined.) If I'm busy taking care of you (and possibly everybody) when do I have time or energy to get my own needs met?

Grieving my ungrieved hurts, losses and traumas

When I got hurt, lost something big or was traumatized, was I allowed to express my pain and even grieve? If your answer is "no" then you were traumatized twice, the first time by a trauma and then when you weren't allowed to express your pain. It helps to revisit some of the old traumas from our childhood if we are still getting memories back of them and let ourselves feel the feelings around the trauma that we weren't allowed to feel back then. That's how we release these old traumas. We don't have to figure them out at the start, just feel the associated feelings, name things accurately and eventually let go of our unhealthy attachment to them.

Difficulty giving love, and difficulty receiving love

Seriously, how many AFGEs have you experienced around trying to give and get love? If your answer is "too many!" then exploring these core issues is going to help you by first learning to love yourself. And then we will know what we want and it will be a lot healthier than what has gone on before.

TABLE OF LEVELS, CONSEQUENCES AND ATTENTION NEEDED TO HELP SOLVE CONFLICTS IN AN AFGE

Level	Threats & Consequences	Attention*	Possible Lessons Learned
5	Life threatening	Total focus required	• Sort out or prioritize each conflict's seriousness.
4	**Major** loss *probable*	Near total focus	• If a low threat, identify & address any of the nine triggering factors as discussed in *Wisdom to Know the Difference.*
3	Major loss *possible*, but unlikely	More as needed to prevent the loss	
2	**Minor** loss *probable*	Some as needed	• Use a combined mental & spiritual approach to resolve conflict.
1	Minor loss *possible*, but unlikely	Little	
0	Inconsequential	Little or none	• Remember & repeat the Serenity Prayer when needed.

*For all conflict levels, gathering **more information** usually helps resolve it.

How Threatening is my Current Upset?

In his book *Wisdom to Know the Difference*,[11] Charles Whitfield shows us how to prioritize the triggers in a conflict, upset or AFGE (see Table on previous page). Study this table and consider using it in your next AFGE.

On page 29 he writes, "Before recovery, many of us may have used an all-or-none approach to handle our conflicts. We fight or attack the other party. Or we may run away, withdraw, hide or decline to engage them in working through our differences. While some minor conflicts may be appropriately and successfully mostly ignored, the most efficient approach is usually to face it head-on, engage the other party as needed and work it through."

Control is another common core issue in AFGEs. When we recognize that we have no control over most things, that we only have control over ourselves, our actions and reactions, we begin to learn to let go of old traumas, stories and painful emotions. We heal.

Being able to realize and name a core issue is one of the most important things we can do to create a life that is balanced and in harmony. If you review the list of core issues it is obvious that we need to learn how to be balanced, to learn when to let go. Knowing what our core issues are helps us to understand what to do in order to change our default mode to something positive and joyful. Living a life that is wise requires a certain amount of discipline and self-study. We will discuss these in the next part.

In his books, talks and private practice, Charles Whitfield talks about "getting down on the floor and wrestling" with the pain of AFGEs associated with these core issues.

This emphasizes the importance of experientially working through our painful feelings in any upset. We think this metaphor

---

11 Whitfield C 2012 *Wisdom to Know the Difference: Core issues in Relationships, Recovery and Living.* Muse House Press, Atlanta, GA

is an important one to remember. It's not easy, but the rewards are plentiful.

Sharon: Barbara's above summary of major core issues is a helpful tool in beginning to deal with an AFGE. When we know just what issue or problem is really bothering us we can begin the healing process. We all have deep-seated issues that we are usually unaware of. We have expended a great deal of effort to keep them hidden and repressed because we really don't want to deal with them. But, here's the bad news: we have to deal with them in order to live a fulfilled life. Bad news is always followed by good news: there is a way to do it.

We can change from living our life where we are unaware of our ego and Real Self or Soul to living where we become aware of when we are oriented towards one or the other. Identifying the core issue in an AFGE is the first step. Then we slowly peel it apart, layer by layer, until we are staring at the center– that dark void we fear– and we discover that we can live to tell about it. When we expose our fear to light, it melts, just like what happened with the Wicked Witch.

Here are a few things that I use when I need to uncover just what an AFGE is trying to tell me.

1. **Listen**. Listen to all those upsetting thoughts that are crashing around in my head and question them. I question them intently. What does this thought mean that "everything is awful." The truth is that everything is not awful. I have food, shelter and friends, people who love me. So what exactly is awful? What specifically is the "awful" or fearsome part?

2. Now we can begin to dissect this AFGE. We have to **name** the "awful" stuff. "Awful" may be that someone we love and care about is in emotional or physical pain. Or perhaps a trusted friend has hurt you. The list of "awful" can be long. But at the center of the AFGE there is usually a core issue (or several core issues) that we have to face. What am I afraid of? What am I angry at or about? What is the core

issue? Referring to the list above will help us zero in on the true source of our AFGE. Once we face it and give it a name we can then start to understand the situation. Then we can begin the healing process.

3. When we are dealing with the **reality** of a situation without stories or fantasies of what we *think* is going on, we move out of a childlike reaction into an adult response. And when we stop building stories, creating fantasies in our minds of what we think may be going on we find ourselves living with more contentment and peace. This is the gift of an AFGE. It is a source of deep inner growth.

PART 2

Coming Into Wisdom

Naming and working through an AFGE creates a new way of looking at old beliefs and current upsets.

Learning and practicing these new ways of looking creates wisdom over time.

Challenging what we have believed and done in each AFGE helps us grow.

Incorporating this growth into our everyday life gives us wisdom.

CHAPTER 6

Natural Meditation

Sharon: One of the most important things to understand about doing meditation is to keep it friendly. Meditation can be our best friend, a place to rest from the stressors of a fast-paced life. Seated on a cushion or in a chair with nowhere else to be, with nothing else to do, meditation gives you permission to let your heart, mind and soul find a few moments of peace. Meditation is not just for people who can sit in a lotus position and chant "OM." Meditation is for all of us, and it is much more than just sitting.

Meditation and prayer are somewhat similar and yet different. It has been said that prayer is when we are talking to God and meditation is when we are listening. That voice we are listening to is our deepest Self, the part of us that is always there, the part that is connected to all other living beings. But meditation can also be something we do while we are cleaning the house, watering the lawn or doing the dishes.

Here is an example of meditation while fully engaged in the present moment. Recently I was at a local fair. It was a perfect New England day, with a great blue sky, warm sun and the smell of green grass filling the air. The fair was crowded, and while everything was fine, I could feel only the pressure of all the people around me and the deep, dull pain that had surfaced in my back. I had done too much walking uphill and my injured back complained. I was cranky, sweaty and thinking only about getting back to the car. Then a woman stepped right in front of me, almost knocking me over. I felt my irritation grow and was ready to say something snarky when I felt a soft touch on my leg. I looked down to see two very brown eyes in a very small body look up at me as he danced on his hind legs, tail wagging, smiling his dog smile. Everything around me disappeared, the noise, the pain, the irritation, as I reached down and scooped him up. An eight-week-old rescue Yorkshire Terrier/Maltese mix puppy wanted my full attention– he wanted to lean into me and connect, to touch and be friends. He was curiosity in fur as he jumped and rolled around on the new grass. He was a teacher to me, letting me see again how beautiful the world is when I open my eyes and heart to it.

When I left I was smiling and my back pain had lifted. I pondered this incident. Just what is it about puppies, babies or any young animal that touches us? What is it that releases us from our everyday concerns and lets us enter into complete connection with another? As I thought about it I came to the conclusion that what happens in these moments is that we let our hearts open and we let go of our individual self (or our ego) and enter into that cosmic arena of interconnection.

Most animals seem to live by instinct, but we have big brains and an intellect, with available philosophy, religion, mathematics and all the technology of our modern life. But along with this capacity for higher thinking we lost our deep contact with the bliss of existence. When I was gently stroking that small puppy it created an opening within me. I was aware afterwards (not during, because I truly was "in the moment") of feeling a lightness, that my back no longer hurt. There was a flow of energy in and around me that was natural, and that is how we feel when we are in touch with who we really are. It was a deeply meaningful AFGE, and I'm grateful to that small dog for reminding me how to just "be." Not all AFGEs are big upsets. Many are gentle wake-up calls from our Soul to see the beauty around us.

That is one form of meditation. Being aware. In the moment. That's it. No mystery or special tools needed. Just me and my attention. In the here and now.

Buddhists sometimes use the term "emptiness" to describe this state. It is a word that we as Westerners misunderstand. Just what the heck is meant by emptiness other than disappearing?

What the deeper meaning of emptiness brings to us is how to be open, to let go of all preconceptions and beliefs we have had–to open the heart, mind and intellect to all the incredible possibilities that are out there in the world and inside of each of us–to receive and experience without making a judgment–*to be empty so we can be filled.* Filled with something new, something that may change us, or at the very least, create a new way of seeing and thinking.

Emily Dickinson said it so beautifully in a line from one of her poems: "I dwell in possibility. "

Think about that. Dwelling in possibility! How fantastic that feeling would be if we could only let go of what we think has to be, must be or has always been the "way we do things."   Part of self-inquiry is finding a way to freedom. Freedom from the ideas we have always had about how we have to act, think or express. Once we begin to question and look for our inner truth we feel the burden of others' opinions and expectations drop away. We find an openness and liberation previously undiscovered. We begin to really live, to find that peace and happiness that has eluded us for so long.

So how do we really do this, where do we begin? I think one of the most helpful ways is to just be still. And you don't have to sit on a cushion or close your eyes. But closing the eyes does help to filter out visual stimulation so we can focus more clearly on the inner stuff. And it can be a circus in there! At first all you will hear is a clamor of voices, each seeking to be in the front row, each raising their hand and jumping around like the know-it-all kid in school. But if you don't point to any one in particular, just let them fight it out, eventually they do get tired and settle down. All but a few remain and those few have been quiet, sitting in the back hoping you would overlook them. Because those few thoughts, hopes and questions are the ones we need to hear and to understand. That's why all learning traditions ask us to sit still, to go inside because that is where the answers lie to all of our difficulties and dissatisfaction. They aren't outside of us, they reside right here in us. And we are the only ones who have the relationship with them and the power to change them.

For a moment let's try a simple exercise, a meditation to calm our mind. Meditation is first about letting us get in touch with the ability we have to let go of stress and tension. Read through the next paragraph first and then do the exercise.

Sit comfortably in a chair with your back straight, no slumping. A straight back helps us breathe more efficiently and keeps us from falling asleep. First take a deep breath in and then let it out with a sigh. Make some noise so your body knows you are relaxing. Do that again, and then one more time. Three deep full breaths that are let out with a sigh help us let go of tension in the mind as well as the body. It triggers the relaxation response in the nervous system, and the body feels it and welcomes it. Now sit up a little straighter and let your breath deepen on each inhale and exhale. Spend a few moments just simply breathing, let your ears be open to the sounds around you, but don't focus on any one sound, just let them flow around you until you really don't hear them. And breathe. That's it. Nothing else. Then open your eyes.

That was pretty simple, wasn't it? But how do you feel right now? A little softer, less tense? You might even have a smile on your face. This is the way we can feel most of the time once we begin to learn the value of sitting down with ourselves.

Recently I taught a recovery group at a conference near the beach. Most of the people attending had never meditated, thinking it was too difficult for them, so I suggested we do a walking meditation on the beach. I asked everyone to enter this practice with awareness. In other words, to be aware of the feel of sand under their feet, to hear the waves, the sounds of birds overhead and feel the soft salt air on their face, but to not think about it. Just observe. I asked that they walk in solitude so they could be fully "there." That was it. Nothing complicated. Just walking and being. We did this for twenty minutes and then broke for lunch.

When I rang the chime to end the meditation, many kept walking. They were completely content to be there on the beach and to be in the freedom of the moment.

There is no right or wrong way to meditate, there are no set rules as to how long you should spend doing "nothing." It is all up to us. What meditation does is help us to train our mind to rest in its natural state, free from the hurdy-gurdy noise of thoughts and emotions, free of to-do lists, free of judgments. We don't actually stop thinking (mostly impossible, since our minds are programmed to "think"), but we don't follow the thoughts. When sitting in meditation and the thought "I'm hungry" jumps in, you just note it and let it go. We don't follow "I'm hungry" with *"I'll have some peanut butter when I finish meditating....maybe I'll have a sandwich instead.....last time I had a sandwich it was at the deli.....I really like the color of the walls in the deli....maybe I should paint my bedroom that color...."* blah blah blah.... and we are off and running on a Thought-Train-to-Nowhere. If we don't follow that original thought there will be several moments of just peaceful quiet in our mind before another thought jumps in. But by not following our thoughts we have many more moments of quiet and have calmed the chaos within for a little while. When we step back into our busy life we will usually feel more centered and less harried.

This can be accomplished with just ten minutes a day. It can change our lives. For in those few quiet moments we will hear the voice of our Soul calling us inward to just rest and be content. That's what the group was feeling during the walking meditation on the beach, contentment and peace.

CHAPTER 7

Necessary Traits For the Path to Inner Peace

Barbara: For me, the biggest trait for getting on the path to inner peace is humility. We have defined humility as the willingness and openness to learn more about self, others, and if we choose, a Higher Power.

While writing the book *The Power of Humility*[12] , Charlie and I realized that humility can be broken down into twelve characteristics. They are **having:** 1) openness, 2) an attitude of "don't know," 3) curiosity, 4) innocence, 5) a child-like nature, 6) spontaneity, 7) spirituality, 8) tolerance, 9) patience, 10) integrity, 11) detachment, and 12) letting go — all of which lead to inner peace and what we called **Level 3 — Co-Creation**. In this level of functioning our creativity is free- flowing.

What happened next in our writing process surprised us. There were two more principles of humility that came through — not intellectually like the ones above — but in a creative way that was purely **Co-Creation**.

These principles are *gratitude* and *"being nobody special."* I knew about gratitude, but "being nobody special" surprised me, and I had to search my own Soul (and battle my ego) to find other avenues to convince me to write about it.

---

12 Whitfield C, Whitfield B, Prevatt J, Park R (2006). *The Power of Humility: Choosing Peace Over Conflict in Relationships*. Health Communications, Inc. Deerfield Bch, FL

"Being Nobody Special"

If our developmental process is healthy, we start out as ego-attached or "somebody special," and then work through a cycle during our lives to become someone who is ego-detached or "nobody special." It is in that nobody-special-ness that we can be anybody. Fatigue, neurosis, anxiety, or fear all come from identifying with the somebody-special-ness. But we have to start somewhere. It does seem that we have to be somebody before we can be nobody. If we started out being nobody at the beginning of this incarnation, we probably wouldn't have made it this far. It's that force of somebody- specialness that develops the social and physical survival mechanisms. It's only now, having evolved to this point that we learn to put that somebody- specialness, that whole survival kit, which we called the ego, into perspective.

At first we really "think" we've lost something. It's a while before we can appreciate the peace that comes from the simplicity of no-mind, of just emptiness, of not having to be somebody all the time. For when we become nobody there is no tension, no pretense, no one trying to be anyone or anything. The natural state of the mind shines through unobstructed, The natural state of the mind is pure love, pure awareness. We've cleared away all of our mind trips that kept us being who we thought we were. [13]

In a society where everybody has to be somebody special, what a joy it can be to walk along and be nobody special. It is freeing, peaceful and serene. We learn to listen and hear. And where we are when we are nobody special is in the heart of our True Self (or Soul.)

Our True Self is the source of our creative abilities. It explores the depth of our creativity by tapping into the energy of what some call "Our Higher Self," Atman, guardian angel, Christ Consciousness, Ruach ha Kadosh, Buddha Nature, etc.

---

13 Whitfield et al 2006 *The Power of Humility: Choosing Peace over Conflict in Relationships.* Muse House Press, Atlanta, GA.

Our ego wants us to be special. It wants us to focus on keeping it inflated. Our ego also is the seat of writer's block. Our True Self flows with our creative process as long as we keep reminding our ego that we are *nobody special.*

Sharon: No matter how we may struggle or strive in this life, we cannot be happy without peace and contentment. And to experience these we may need to let go of our wants, desires and attachments. When we strive to always be someone special, to be perfect, we are keeping our real self from being happy. Happiness *is* contentment. When we are at ease and in the flow of our life, we are living in contentment. When we drop out of that flow, we are then living in unease. Barbara listed twelve plus two traits that are essential to our inner well-being. Yoga tells us that we need to cultivate living as a wise person would live in order to be free of unnecessary desires and discontents. One of the most important things we can do is to recognize that we are in charge of how we react to situations. As we become more aware we learn that we have the ability to choose how we *experience* life. The Dalai Lama said: "There is always pain in life, it is up to us to chose how long we suffer."

How do we connect to that contentment? We usually need to stop and find a stillness within us to contemplate where and when we left the path of peacefulness. Sometimes we have no choice—we lose a job, a loved one, or we become ill. These things can short-circuit our contentment, so we need to find another path that we can travel that will bring us back once more to that inner quiet we need. When we stop pushing away what has brought us discontent/upset/an AFGE (e.g., the lost job, grief, illness, etc.) and accept where we are in this moment, we then begin the process of changing it. Our lives involve change. Nothing stays the same. When we are faced with a difficult time, an AFGE, we can learn resilience. We can learn to control our response to painful events. One trait that can help us respond and recover is to stay connected to others and not isolate ourselves when we are in need of comfort.

Another way to peace is to get up and do something: walk, run, read a book. Volunteer to help in an animal shelter or a clinic. Focusing on helping others will give us a better perspective on our own lives.

Meditation has always been one of those things that can help us regain our peace. When we take the time to sit, we are actually training our mind to settle down, to let go of chaos and be quiet so we can really think and see the real glory of life that is always around us. Meditation, self-inquiry and contemplation are what help us access contentment. When we are quiet we can learn to let go of those thoughts that are bringing us discontent and learn to accept where we are in this moment.

Gratitude

One practice we can cultivate everyday and benefit from is the practice of gratitude. When we take the time to assess what we have in life we usually are surprised by the abundance. One of the most important things I have learned is that my mental attitude is formed by my own thoughts. I create those thoughts and I also create my emotions, moods and attitudes that go with them. Years ago, when I was in the middle of a particularly bad AFGE and feeling so unsure of where my life was going, I was lying in bed unable to sleep. Scary thoughts of poverty and unemployment were dancing in my head, when all of a sudden a clear strong voice in my head said "Stop—life is so much more than this. There were at least five things today that were good, name them!" So I began to list five things and quickly found many more. That was the beginning of my gratitude practice, and I have never stopped my list. Sometimes I write them down, other times I silently recite them in my heart. Try keeping a notebook with you and write down your own thoughts on your gratefulness. It helps to keep us centered on the really important things in life.

There will be times when we find it difficult to feel gratitude, especially in times of great sorrow and loss, but if we move beyond our immediate pain and find our inner source of compassion and strength, humbly acknowledging the blessings we do have with gratitude, it can help us cross over the bridge of pain or sorrow.

So when Barbara and I are mentioning that we feel grateful for all that we have, it is more than just our material possessions we are talking about. I am definitely grateful for the shelter, food and security I have because I realize that much of the world suffers and goes without these in varying degrees. Not to acknowledge the basic gifts of food, shelter and security would be narrow-minded. A gratitude practice reminds us to be thankful, to appreciate what we do have. It reinforces our connection to the Universe and to others. With the regular practice of gratitude we become happier, less depressed and more content. As we practice gratitude we will discover that we have an increased sense of purpose in our life.

CHAPTER 8

Natural Spirituality

Barbara:

In the 1971 movie *Harold and Maude,* the two main characters exchange the following dialogue:

Harold: Maude, do you pray?

Maude: No. I communicate.

Harold: With God?

Maude: With Life!

Maude brings up an excellent point about prayer. We were taught in our traditional religions that praying is talking to/asking God. The conversation is flowing *from us to* a Supreme Being. Current writings on spirituality explain how to communicate *both ways* with a Higher Power, or what we naturally perceive as something greater than ourselves - our own "God of Our Understanding."[14]

If we pay attention to our life, as Maude suggests, we perceive an answer coming back to us. Then, our natural spirituality allows us our own interpretation.

I would like to propose a new genre of expanding spirituality because of the new research that is proving that we as a species are evolving beyond where we were before and because I witness this expansion in myself, my colleagues, my friends and in

---

14 Whitfield C et al 2006, *The Power of Humility.* Health Communications, Inc. Deerfield Bch, FL.
    Whitfield B 2009, *The Natural Soul.* Muse House Press, Atlanta, GA.

my counseling practice. Here is some background information to address what is happening within the genre of spirituality, including its current findings, scientific research and publications.

At the University of Connecticut Medical School, my colleagues and I interviewed hundreds of people who had near-death experiences, and we witnessed living proof that religion and spirituality can harmoniously enhance each other. This new expanding spirituality can stand alone in a well-balanced peaceful life -- what this book is all about. It's our choice how to live our life with self, others and God.

We showed that the joyful emotions and sense of connection experienced in a near-death state create changes in a person's life that are long lasting. After a near-death experience there is an earthy realness to how NDErs relate to their life. Their needs for materialism and prestige diminish and they turn to altruistic goals. They change jobs because they are looking for meaning in their lives, and they are driven to share unconditional love. Many grieve if that is impossible in their existing relationships and have to move on.

Some of us wrote books about our near-death experiences and our changes afterwards. Some of the researchers who wrote books admitted how they were changed by their research and their contact with NDErs. What we have observed and documented over time in our writings can be viewed as a new genre where we described all the positive emotions of our NDEs and a direct connection to our selves and our Higher Power. Most of the publishers categorized and labeled our books as "New Age."

Spirituality and the "New Age" long were lumped together. I propose a separation between the two. The New Age is really old spiritual philosophy reframed so that some of us can understand it better. However, over time some charlatans have moved in (as they have in other movements). They capture their audiences with charismatic personalities and aren't evolved enough to balance their ego with their new found or invented wisdom. They can sound narcissistic to many who criticize and are turned off by what they mistakenly see as "New Age." Some even teach and preach psychic abilities as the end all when that is just a development that may happen along the way. Somewhere in this confusion, people become psychic magnets for others' painful emotions because few are talking or writing about healthy boundaries. [15] Lately, a few of these authors and self-made gurus have turned to materialism as their agenda: how to get more stuff, more money, and the like.

New Discoveries in Neuroscience

Harvard psychiatrist George Vaillant continues this theme by defining spirituality first as not being about ideas, sacred texts and theology. He proposed that eight positive emotions: awe, love, trust/faith, compassion, gratitude, forgiveness, joy and hope constitute what we mean by spirituality. He writes in his book *Spiritual Evolution: A Scientific Defense of Faith*, "Spirituality is about emotion and social connection." Much of his data comes from a Harvard study that prospectively charted the lives of 824 men and women for over 60 years. Dr. Vaillant concludes:

"Spirituality is virtually indistinguishable from these positive emotions and is, thus, rooted in our evolutionary biology. Because these emotions are also the same ones for which most religions strive, spirituality is a common denominator for all faiths." [16]

Neuroscientist Andrew Newberg from the University of PA Medical School used functional imaging (fMRI), positron emission tomography (PET scans) and single photon emission computed tomography (SPEC7) to demonstrate that spirituality lies in the limbic system of the brain. Both religion and "New Age" writing usually activate the neocortex where we think in words. The

---

15 See section on Spiritual Bypass in Whitfield B 1995. *Spiritual Awakenings.* Health Communications, Inc Deerfield Bch, FL.
Whitfield, C et al 2006. *The Power of Humility.* Health Communications, Inc. Deerfield Bch, FL.
16 Vaillant G. (2008) *Spiritual Evolution: A Scientific Defense of Faith*

limbic system is where we feel the positive emotions and our positive relationships with others. This area activated by these positive feelings increase our parasympathetic activity producing relaxation, followed by a profound sense of serenity. So writing about theology is located in our neocortex where we are once removed from the experience and the feeling. This new genre of spirituality goes to the limbic system where we feel first hand what the writer is conveying.

Newberg studied Tibetan Buddhists who practiced Kundalini Yoga meditation and had been meditating for many years. He showed that when these meditators achieve a state of mystical union, followed by a profound sense of calm, that the activities of those parts of the neocortical brain were functionally cut off from the rest of the brain. At the same time, both the limbic hippocampus and amygdala were more active. Newberg's subjects meditated on a spiritual symbol or a positive emotion. Some focused on the feeling of forgiveness. He found that the area activated by these positive feelings increases their parasympathetic activity, producing relaxation, followed by a profound sense of serenity. There are no words used in this experience, only a sense of positive or joyful feelings.

Newberg suggests that experiential spirituality reflects "limbic questions" about love, community, positive emotions, and the feeling of "being one with the universe." He has also reported that for meditating nuns, "while in prayer, their sense of God becomes physiologically real," and the meditating Buddhists caught a glimpse of what for them was "an absolute reality."[17]

A New Genre of Expanding Spirituality

Both Dr. Vaillant and Dr. Newberg's work supports this new genre that takes the reader into a feeling state that is experiential in the respect that the brain is picturing or feeling it.

---

17 Newberg Andrew. Personal communication

What we are describing in the above scientific research validates this new definition of spirituality and it's increasing understanding within our evolving biology. There is a powerful link between stimulating the parasympathetic nervous system of the limbic area of the brain and our immune system. Joyful emotions and a loving connection to our self, others, including our community, and God can boost our immunity so that we become physically healthier. What this all means is that there is a new spirituality emerging that is actually part of our biology. We are evolving toward a more naturally spiritual human race and medical research is helping us realize that. We could even hypothesize that becoming physically healthier because of a chain reaction that strengthens our immune system means that this will enhance the spiritual nature of humans by natural selection.

In *Heading Toward Omega: In Search of the Meaning of the Near-Death Experience* Social Psychologist Kenneth Ring hypothesized a new evolutionary step for humans. He called this new evolutionary development "The Omega Prototype." That book came out in 1984. Twenty-eight years later, this science could be validating his theory.

Thus, the new genre of expanding spirituality is the generic umbrella term for our own intimate personal relationship with our self, others and our Higher Power. (Whitfield 2006, 2009). This gives all of us a new opening into a richer, deeper and more evolved way to express the Mystery of our existence.

The joyful feelings, emotions and attitudes of true spirituality take us from focusing on ourselves to compassion for all of life. Our writing can even reflect our deepest experiences by describing emotionally our spirituality through our inner life.

In the Appendix are three poems, one that I wrote and two of Sharon's to explain natural spirituality. In it, we are hoping to explain the earthy realness of this new genre.

Sharon: When we embark on a spiritual path, the journey will naturally take us inward to the essence of who we are. Here in the inner space of our hearts we look at what we consider our deepest values, what meanings we live by. Spirituality emphasizes the practice of loving-kindness, compassion, patience, tolerance; it requires us to be responsible, to live in harmony and balance with others. We cultivate moral integrity and live by a code of non-harming. Spirituality does not belong only to religious communities or churches, it belongs to all of us in whatever way we chose to express it.

In his book, *The Perennial Philosophy*, Aldous Huxley wrote of his belief that all peoples, modern and primitive, have the same essential need to act and live from the foundation of the Soul, to recognize Divine Reality. All faiths and philosophies, from Buddhism to Wiccan have the following words in some form or another as the basis of their ethical beliefs: Do unto others as you would have others do unto you. This is the essence of natural spirituality.

Sacredness is necessary and essential to all of us in order to be fulfilled as human beings. When we look up at a clear night sky, filled with thousands upon thousands of stars and the potential for other life to exist, we can only be filled with awe and wonder. Our Soul yearns to understand the Universe, even though it is beyond our capacity, and this knowledge is where we enter into the miracle of the All. We know we can't comprehend our beginnings or our end. But we trust that there is something bigger and more beautiful in the Universe than what we can see with our eyes. We use the eternal space of our Soul to cultivate love and kindness for others. Loving-kindness is the manifestation of our Soul and this is the state we return to when we leave our body: Eternal, All-encompassing Love.

We each need to create our personal idea of Natural Spirituality, and it should include whatever feels true to each of us. If the faith we were introduced to as children supports our Inner Source, it is right for us. If it doesn't, then consider beginning to search and seek your own path. When we question old beliefs we are not rejecting, but instead reaffirming what we need and feel is right and true for our own growth.

CHAPTER 9

Changing our Perspective: Growing into the AFGE Experience

Sharon: One of those ways of creating our own pathway is to change and/or challenge our perspectives. We may have grown up with families that had "group" perspectives and we automatically believed them. Most of these group perspectives were prejudices such as: we don't frequent places like that, they are dirty; we don't mingle with those types, they are bad; we don't believe in their faith, they are wrong; we don't eat that kind of food, etc. The list of such human admonitions, prejudice and bias is long and ancient. But we can change that in ourselves by the very simple act of questioning. We can increase our ability to see things (emotions and situations) in their true relation to one another.

Our perceptions create our reality. Some 2500 years ago the Buddha said "Our thoughts create our world." We truly are what we think, so taking that as the First Truth, we need to look deeply at all the judgments we make and all the beliefs we have in our personal world.

When we're lost in pain, confusion and doubt, rather than seeing our situation the way we have been conditioned to react, or as we want to see it, we need to step back, breathe and consider that reality may be something different from what we had initially determined. I used to tell my son when he came home from school distraught about something that had happened that day, "Where does this fit on a scale of 1 to 10? Ten being the worst thing and one being a momentary blip." Usually, when he really thought about it, when he let the emotion tied to it go, he would realize that whatever it was really fit in on the very low end. It was a wonderful way for him to learn perspective. He

65

learned to stand back and look it over. (See the table in Chapter Five on Levels in an AFGE). That doesn't mean that this happens quickly, sometimes you have to break it down, or as mentioned previously "get down on the floor and wrestle with it." Developing perspective is an art that takes awareness and determination. Meditation can help us to develop our skill of perception by letting us sit with a problem and become open to our inner source of wisdom that can lead to a resolution.

What we need to learn to do is to be fully and consciously aware of the **reality** of the situation because our perceptions will make us create a reality that isn't all fact but mostly fiction. Anais Nin, writer and poet, stated: "We don't see things as they are, we see them as *we* are." I put the emphasis on the word *we* in her statement because it is the important point. We create our reality. So if we create it, we control it and we can change it. We can take unwholesome thoughts and turn them into wholesome thoughts.

Perception uses all our senses, feelings, ideas, thoughts and beliefs in creating a judgment. We use perception to connect to the world. So the actual or factual aspect of a perception can be camouflaged by our own past experiences. If a current perspective (or AFGE) mimics a childhood trauma, we are likely to respond just as we did as a child. We will group this current experience with the old situation and we will see in it what we previously saw as a child—and we will fail to apply discernment. We will suffer as we did then, and we will not likely change for the better. We will revert to the "default mode" that we developed as a child.

But if instead of reacting, we reflect and review, using an attitude of gentle detachment, we can change and develop our ability to discern. We will no longer continue to react but we will learn to respond. There are no right or wrong perceptions, only incorrect interpretations. We can learn to modify and adjust our ways of thinking.

Going back to Barbara's situation in the introduction, at the time of the betrayal, she felt that it was a ten. But as she describes, she sat with it and even got down on the floor and wrestled with it until she developed perspective and finally turned it over to a Higher Power because she finally got tired of it and didn't want to carry it anymore.

The perspective was brought home a few days later when Barbara's daughter Beth became critically ill. Suddenly what happened before became unimportant–it became a 1 on the scale of 1-10. Now, she was drowning in fear and worry for her child. This was most definitely a ten. And then to further make sure she knew it was a ten, on the way to the hospital the day after Beth's emergency surgery, a AAA tow truck smashed into the rear-end of her car. Part of Barbara's intuitive wisdom when the collision happened was to let the emotional tempest inside her out by screaming and letting her body release the shock in a shaking release. By the time the other driver came out (he must have been stunned too) and she got out of her car, her body had expressed itself so she had no lingering physical pain.

Perspective: This accident didn't really register on the scale of 1 to 10 because her daughter's health was a ten and this was just a blip.

Perspective: At a certain point in Beth's health crisis, Barbara took her worry as a ten down to an eight as she reasoned that it could be worse and Beth was on the mend. The other betrayal dilemma described in the introduction, became a one and then fell off the scale entirely. During the time Beth's illness was a ten, she called me every night to let me hear her feelings and fears. She felt like she was dumping but in fact, was releasing a lot of stress. I didn't need to share any advice with her. I needed to listen and I did. That's what friends are for.

Part of learning to understand just how we perceive a situation is the use of self-inquiry. This is a useful technique that yoga calls for in learning how to live wisely. In this process we learn who we are, what we believe in and what we want to do with our lives. This isn't done in one afternoon. It usually takes a lifetime of looking inward. Sometimes we will laugh out loud at our fears and pretentions. Other times we will softly hold the wounded child that we were. And through this holding and learning we become who we are meant to be.

Barbara: As I read Sharon's words above, I had to laugh about the AAA tow truck. In fact, I remember laughing almost immediately. I could do that because of the few minutes I gave myself to pound the steering wheel and scream and shake. I know enough about releasing acute stress to have given myself permission to let my body go and address itself. I had been pent up over my daughter's surgery the day before, and this was a big thump (actually) to tell me to let myself go. This was not premeditated. My body reacted in a totally spontaneous way.

And when the driver of the truck finally came over, after I got out of my car, he said to me, "Why did you stop?" I had to laugh as I said, "Because the car ahead of me stopped for this light we are sitting at!" The laughter kept coming and I knew it was another way to "shake off" the stress.

I even enjoyed it when two police cars came and were attentive to how I was feeling and whether I wanted to go to an emergency room. They even gently talked with me about filing a report so the truck driver would receive a ticket.

I explained to them that all I wanted to do was leave and get to my daughter so I could see how she was. We all said good-bye, including the truck driver, and I with a deep sense of "just another thump on the journey." By the way, the trucking company gladly had my car fixed the next week. It needed a new bumper. And somehow, I knew that that "bump" slowed me down and made my perspective come back.

PART 3

Life is the Ultimate Wake-Up Call

CHAPTER 10

Conclusion

Sharon: So what is the point of this whole book?

It is to recognize that an AFGE, an upsetting growth experience, is a situation where our inner self recognizes an opportunity to learn. It's an inner wake-up call to let go of old habits and thought patterns that limit us. It is a cosmic "2 x 4" to the head. All we need to do is listen carefully. We use our head, heart and Soul to uncover what this new AFGE is trying to tell us. It isn't easy. It takes work on our part but the benefits will lead to more and more possibilities of change.

Another way to think of an AFGE is as a transition, a moving away from one condition in our life that isn't working into a freer, more positive space. An AFGE helps us get "unstuck," to move forward to what we all ultimately want– to be healthy, happy, and content.

Right now, think of something in your life that you want to change, (start with something small rather than leaving your boring job and opening an Indian vegetarian Kosher food restaurant in New York City — there is one there already — really). Remember when we talked earlier about how our thoughts affect us — now put it in motion. Each time our inner voices surface with all the reasons why we can't change, why this won't work — just tell them that they are fired and no longer needed. We are in charge.

To help with the changes and reboot your default mode, include new habits such as moving our bodies more, as in exercise. And for all of us who hate exercise, think about the fact that aerobic activity stimulates the brain's endocannabinoid system, which is where blissed-out moods are waiting, and it also shakes up the opioid system which then sends out feel-good endorphins (as in a runner's high). These two reactions help reduce fear and anxiety and create a sense of satisfaction and calm. And, most important, moving and using our bodies in activities such as walking gives us control over how we feel physically and emotionally.

Another habit is to get outside. Feel the timelessness and scale of nature as it gives us perspective into our daily concerns and worries. Breathe in clean, clear oxygen and breathe out all the negative thoughts. Each full breath we take helps jumpstart our immune system. Plants produce compounds as a defense against bacteria, and when we breathe these in we are helping our own bodies' defenses.

Some say that the purpose of our life is to be happy, to be content with who we are and where we are in the moment. Stop condemning, stop judging and nagging. When we do these things we are dishonoring our best part, the beautiful inner "I." The "I" who loves and cherishes life. The "I" who brings goodness to others. If the "I" is always finding fault with itself, then the True Self cannot do what it is meant to do — flourish.

So Wake Up! Begin today to understand those AFGEs that show up and vanquish them with love and laughter.

Default Outlook

Barbara: For those who were fortunate to have a happy childhood with loving parents and harmony with their sibs (probably less than 20% of us), their "default" (naturally) is peaceful and content. The rest of us (the remaining majority 80%) most likely developed a default that is painful. We need to "reset" our default mode, and handling AFGEs is the road to reset.

Whatever your default mode is, don't believe that it is permanent. There's always a reset button, and that's what this book is really all about.

Sharon and I both wish you the best default mode that we human beings can experience. It's our birthright. It's what we are here to discover. Along the way we will grow and evolve. And we hope that this book is your doorway into a world of love and joy — in your inner life and your outer world.

Sharon K. Cormier

Barbara Harris Whitfield

February, 2013

APPENDIX

Barbara's poem:
Doorway

When the sun is setting behind the trees
And the mugginess of an August day is
Hanging on for one last hour,
I sit on our porch and wait for
The "I" in me to disappear.

My doorway to spirituality is a simple prayer,
"Here I am God with open hands."
As I look at my hands opening,
I release all the tensions and identities of the day.
Wife
Mother
Grandmother
Writer
Therapist
Melt into "nobody special."

I watch giant pines, oaks and beeches
Swaying in the breeze.
I respect them for their age,
And, the way they radiate the peace
That can come with growing old.

The slow fan overhead gently moves away
The sticky heat and dampness
As my awareness floats into a meditation
On the swaying of the trees as they engage the wind.
These trees perform a sacred dance with the spirit of the
breeze.
The porch is a shelf for that little spark of me that is still left

And transformed into the Witness -
To witness the Universe in my piece of the world.
And to witness my peace in the world.

I melt into the Eternal Now.

These moments bring serenity and sometimes awe.
Beyond comprehension but
Within the reach of a fleeting perception.

These moments out of time...

Remind us of our blessed connection.
And bring us contentment and gratitude.

Sharon's poems:
Being here and now

A finch came with a song today

he sat on the sill

filled the house with

clear pulsing notes

until nothing else was there

only his chant

then it entered me and

I became weightless sound

without form, empty of all

except the song.

The Blue Heron

In the field, by the pond

      stands a blue heron

            his back to the early sun

wings held half open

      a hieroglyphic

            against the blue sky

I wait with him

      watching his naked prayer

            asking nothing of no One

just complete acceptance of

      warmth from a distant star

            on wet feathers

            amen

REFERENCES AND RECOMMENDED READING

Near-Death and other Spiritually Transformative Experiences

Newberg A, D'Aquili E, and Rause V (2001) *Why God Won't go Away: Brain Science and the Biology of Belief.* Ballantine, New York, NY.

Ring K 1984. *Heading Toward Omega: In Search of the Meaning of the Near–Death Experience.* Quill, NY.

Ring K, Valarino E. 2000. *Lessons from the Light: What We Can Learn from the Near-Death Experience.* Insight Books NY.

Sunfellow D, WEBSITE New Heaven New Earth, Near-Death Experiences   NDE http://nhne-nde.org http://ndestories.org

Whitfield B 1995. *Spiritual Awakenings.* Health Communications, Inc. Deerfield Bch, FL.

Whitfield B 2009. *The Natural Soul: Unity with the Spiritual Energy that connects us to our self, others and God. What It looks like and how It feels.* Muse House Press, Atlanta GA

Recovery and Self Help

Whitfield, C 1986. *Healing the Child Within.* Health Communications, Inc. Deerfield Beach, FL

Whitfield C, Whitfield B, Prevatt J, Park R (2006). *The Power of Humility: Choosing Peace Over Conflict in Relationships.* Health Communications, Inc. Deerfield Bch, FL

Whitfield C 2012 *Wisdom to Know the Difference: Core Issues in Relationships, Recovery and Life*. Muse House Press, Atlanta, GA

Yoga Philosophy:

Cope, Stephen. *Yoga and the Quest for the True Self*.   New York, New York: Bantam Books, 1999.

Cormier, Sharon. *Where the Lotus Blooms*. Atlanta, GA Muse House Press: 2011

Satchidananda, Swami Sri. *The Yoga Sutras of Patanjali*. Yogaville,VA: Integral Yoga Publications, 1978

Buddha Within. New York, New York: Broadway Books, 1997.

Kornfield, Jack.*The Wise Heart: A Guide to the Universal Teachings of Buddhist Psychology*. New York, New York: Bantam Dell: 2008

Meditation:

Yongey Mingyur Rinpoche. *The Joy of Living*. New York, New York:Three Rivers Press, 2007.

Salzberg, Sharon.*Lovingkindness: The Revolutionary Art of Happiness.* Boston, MA: Shambala Publications, Inc. 1995

INDEX

ABOUT THE AUTHORS

Sharon K. Cormier has been practicing and studying Buddhism and yoga for over thirty years. She is a certified yoga therapist, Reiki Master, meditation instructor and workshop leader. She is also on the faculty of Sacred Rivers Yoga Center where she trains new teachers in the philosophy and practice of yoga. She is the creator of an inclusive form of yoga called Wholeness Yoga that is an integration of yin yoga, hatha yoga, Buddhist mindfulness and healing Qigong. She also leads workshops on Loving-Kindness Meditation, a form of meditation that invites us to create a path of loving-kindness in our lives enriching us with natural joy, compassion and inner peace.

Sharon was also a spokesperson for the International Association for Near Death Studies, appearing on The Joan Rivers Show, The Today Show and with Barbara on Larry King Live as well as participating in documentaries on NDE's with the Canadian Broadcasting Company and the Netherlands Broadcasting Co.

She is a poet, writer and inventor with two patents for the Candle Quencher. Her first book, *Where The Lotus Blooms: Finding Inner Peace Through Mindfulness, Yoga and Meditation* was released in 2011 and her poems have been published in several anthologies.

For more information:

shantiyoga.sharon@gmail.com

www.sharonkcormier.com

Barbara Harris Whitfield had a profound near-death experience in 1975 that turned her life into a search for answers. She went back to school and became an ICU respiratory therapist that led her to write and lecture on "The Emotional Needs of Critical Care Patients." Next, she became a researcher in the Department of Psychiatry at the University of Connecticut School of Medicine looking at the psychological, emotional, energetic and spiritual aftereffects of people who have had a near-death experience. She taught classes on these aftereffects at Rutgers University's Institute on Alcohol and Drug Studies for 12 years calling her classes "When the 12th Step happens first." Barbara has appeared on Oprah, Donahue, Larry King Live, CNN Medical News, Bio Channel, and more. She is in private practice in Atlanta, Georgia with Charles Whitfield, MD doing individual and group psychotherapy for adults that were repeatedly traumatized as children.

Barbara is the author or co-author of eight books: *Full Circle: The Near-death experience and Beyond* (Simon and Schuster, Pocket NY, NY 1990), *Spiritual Awakenings* (Health Communications, Inc, Deerfield Beach FL 1995), *Final Passage* (HCI 1998), *The Power of Humility* (HCI with Charles Whitfield 2006), *The Natural Soul* (Muse House Press, Atlanta GA 2010), *Victim to Survivor and Thriver: Carole's Story (*MHP 2011), *Casey Anthony* (Muse House Press with Charles Whitfield MD and Wendy Murphy JD, 2011) and *Timeless Troubadours, The Moody Blues Music and Message* co-authored with Charles Whitfield, March 2013.

Barbara is on the faculty and board of The American Center for the Integration of Spiritually Transformative Experiences (ACISTE) and The Institute for the Study of Empathy in Psychotherapy, Education and Living. She also teaches a module on *Unity as Practice* for The Center for Sacred Studies' program for Ministers of Prayer.

For more information: www.barbarawhitfield.com